East Sussex
SMUGGLERS' PUBS

Terry Townsend

To my wife Carol
for in every sense this is her book, too.

First published in Great Britain in 2018

Copyright © Terry Townsend 2018

All rights reserved. No part of this publication may be reproduced, stored in a retrieval system, or transmitted in any form or by any means without the prior permission of the copyright holder.

British Library Cataloguing-in-Publication Data
A CIP record for this title is available from the British Library

ISBN 978 0 85710 118 1

PiXZ Books
Halsgrove House, Ryelands Business Park,
Bagley Road, Wellington, Somerset TA21 9PZ
Tel: 01823 653777
Fax: 01823 216796
email: sales@halsgrove.com

An imprint of Halstar Ltd, part of the Halsgrove group of companies
Information on all Halsgrove titles is available at: www.halsgrove.com

Printed and bound in India by
Parksons Graphics

CONTENTS

ACKNOWLEDGEMENTS

Thanks go to Robert Smith, Adrienne Bradney-Smith,
and Brenda and Tony Stables for their continued
help with proof reading and suggestions.

Thanks also to Karen Binaccioni for her invaluable design input.

**TERRY TOWNSEND'S OTHER
HALSGROVE TITLES INCLUDE:**

*Once Upon a Pint – A Readers' Guide to the
Literary Pubs & Inns of Dorset & Somerset*

*Dorset Smugglers' Pubs,
More Dorset Smugglers' Pubs,
East Cornwall Smugglers' Pubs: Kingsand to Mevagissey
Hampshire Smugglers' Pubs,
Isle of Wight Smugglers' Pubs,
Kent Smugglers' Pubs,
Suffolk Smugglers' Pubs
West Cornwall Smugglers' Pubs: St Ives to Falmouth*

Bristol & Clifton Slave Trade Trails

*Jane Austen & Bath
Jane Austen's Hampshire
Jane Austen's Kent*

Bibliography

Kent Barker: *The Smuggling Life of Gabriel Tomkins*

Mark Bullen: *Contraband County – Sussex Smuggling in the Nineteenth Century*

Kenneth M. Clark: *Smuggling in Rye and District*

Richard Platt: *Smugglers' Britain*

David Russell: *The Pubs of Hastings & St Leonards 1800 - 2000*

David Russell: *The Pubs of Rye, East Sussex 1750 -1950*

The ancient houses and pubs in Rye are built on undercrofts like this which were
formerly linked by smugglers' tunnels.

Pub Locations

1	Alfriston, *Ye Olde Smugglers Inne*	11	Hooe, *The Red Lion*
2	Boreham Street, *Bull's Head*	12	Iden, *The Bell*
3	Burwash Weald, *The Wheel Inn*	13	Jevington, *The Eight Bells*
4	Burwash, *Rose & Crown*	14	Mayfield, *The Rose & Crown*
5	Coleman's Hatch, *The Hatch Inn*	15	Norman's Bay, *The Star Inn*
6	East Dean, *The Tiger Inn*	16	Pett Village, *Two Sawyers*
7	Groombridge, *The Crown Inn*	17	Pevensey, *The Smugglers*
8	Hastings, *Hastings Arms*	18	Robertsbridge, *The George Inn*
9	Hastings, *The Stag Inn*	19	Rye, *The Mermaid Inn*
10	Hooe, *The Lamb Inn*	20	Whatlington, *The Royal Oak*

Edward I created the climate for the first smugglers by imposing a tax on the export of wool, the most important raw material in the English economy.

Introduction

Before the establishment of a customs system in the twelfth century there were no smugglers as trade was free. In search of new sources of revenue Edward I imposed a tax on the export of wool, the most important raw material in the English economy.

This move created the first smugglers called 'Owlers', and the first conflicts with officials charged with preventing smuggling.

Taking advantage of the proximity to France, Owlers operated mainly in the marshland around Rye, illegally exporting wool and even the prized sheep that grazed the area. The Ypres Castle Inn lurking in the lee of Rye Castle became the smugglers' preferred meeting place.

Within a hundred years, additional duties were imposed but this time on imports of luxury goods such as silks, tea, tobacco and brandy. This move doubled the opportunities and rewards for

Rye 'Owlers' attacking Revenue Men at the beginning of a conflict that lasted 150 years.

Ypres Castle Inn lurking in the lee of Rye Castle was the preferred pub of Rye Owlers.

smugglers, although those involved preferred to call themselves 'free traders'.

By the end of the seventeenth century poor social conditions exacerbated the situation and smuggling became a widespread occupation affecting most Sussex residents in one way or another. Smuggling offered an alternative to poverty. A labourer could earn more in one night helping with a landing than working an entire week in the fields. Finding an adequate workforce to bring the harvest in became a major problem.

By the time of the arrival of the 'Golden Age of Smuggling' (roughly 1750-1830) matt-ers had escalated almost out of control. Smugglers formed themselves into large, highly organised and heavily armed gangs, based near convenient landing places on the coast, like Pevensey and Bexhill, Hastings and Rye.

Those involved in the nefarious activity of smuggling preferred to call themselves 'free traders'.

Gangs were also established at strategically placed inland villages en route to London like Robertsbridge, Mayfield and Groombridge. To avoid recognition smugglers assumed nicknames like 'Nasty Face', Jevington Jig', 'Towzer' and 'Old Joll' etc., and a number were landlords of country inns.

On the quiet sand and shingle beaches of Sussex armed gangs rendezvoused with small boats ferrying contraband from fast Channel-crossing luggers.

Of all the old landing places Cuckmere
Haven remains the most evocative.
Photograph by Baz Edmondson

On the quiet sand and shingle beaches of Sussex armed gangs rendezvoused with small boats ferrying contraband from fast Channel-crossing luggers whose owners traded with French merchants.

Of all the old landing places Cuckmere Haven remains the most evocative. The Blockade Watch House and the later Coastguard cottages still stand guard over an otherwise deserted bay with its notorious smuggling history.

A succession of eighteenth-century foreign wars drained the country's finances and manpower. The insubstantial main force combating smuggling often consisted of older men unsuitable for military service. The life of a land-based

Revenue Officer was hard and poorly rewarded. In consequence bribery and corruption were endemic.

When Preventive forces eventually became more effective smugglers were forced to use comparatively

The insubstantial main force used to combat smuggling often consisted of older men unsuitable for military service.

inaccessible beaches. In the Seven Sisters area derricking was employed as a technique to haul goods up the cliff face. Contraband landed on the beach was stacked in baskets or on some form of pallet – often a farm-gate. Using a horse-driven winch or windlass on the cliff top smugglers hauled up the contraband. Records exist of such happenings at numerous spots, but notably Birling Gap.

The formerly inaccessible beach where derricking was employed as a technique to haul goods up the Birling Gap cliff face.

Men engaged in unloading and conveying contraband inland poss-essed unrivalled knowledge of the terrain. They also held an immense advantage over the forces deployed against them in the support they received from the majority of the country people and enjoyed free access to barns, churches and pubs en route as places of concealment.

By way of example the Groombridge Gang landed goods near The Bo-Peep

pub in Bulverhythe and, employing mules or pack-ponies, transported contraband across two counties to a similarly named pub at Chelsfield in North Kent where they handed on the booty to London gangs. The Bo-Peep nursery rhyme is thought to derive from an old Hastings/St Leonards tale

Table top tombs in Jevington church-yard were used to conceal contra-band en route inland.

The double sided sign on the Bo-Peep pub at Bulverhythe.

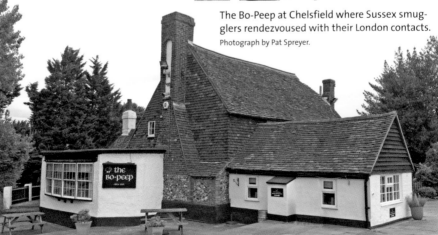

The Bo-Peep at Chelsfield where Sussex smug-glers rendezvoused with their London contacts.
Photograph by Pat Spreyer.

A Royal Navy
Blockade revenue
cutter in pursuit of
a smugglers'
lugger.

and is a metaphor for the hide and seek nature of the relation-
ship between Revenue Men and smugglers. Customs Officers
are always searching and peeping while smugglers slip by
carrying their contraband behind them.

In 1821 the National Coastguard Service was introduced with
cottages built at regular points around the coast to house the
men and their families. This disciplined and uniformed body

Eventually each
port had a
Customs House
Collector. Twenty-
eight officers were
supervised from
this former
Custom House at
Rye.

consisted of shore-based patrols, a rowing guard offshore and Revenue cutters patrolling the sea.

In time each port had a Customs House Collector supported by other officers ranging from his deputy down to boatmen. By 1822 there were twenty-eight such officers in Rye alone, which suggests the scale of the whole smuggling enterprise. In the war against smuggling the initiative had passed from the smuggler.

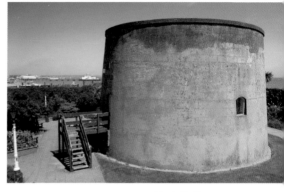

Martello Towers like this at Eastbourne were originally built to combat the threat of invasion by Napoleon's army and later utilised as Coast Blockade stations.

Peace finally came to Britain in June 1815 with the defeat of Napoleon and many service men returned home to deprived rural areas of the south east. The government, fearful of a return to the smuggling heyday of thirty years earlier, now had resources to set up a naval cordon. By 1824 the 'Blockade Line' which stretched 200 miles around the coastline from Sheerness to Chichester was manned by three-thousand officers and men.

The greatest factor in the final suppression of smuggling in the first half of the nineteenth century was the reduction or abolition of most of the duties as part of the Free Trade policy. With the wholesale reform of the Customs Service in 1853, which ensured a loyal and efficient force, the picture was completed. Smuggling, thereafter, was relatively unimportant. The Coastguards remained, but their work became more of a sea rescue and life-saving service.

The Smugglers' Pub

In many cases the local inn became the smugglers' centre of operations where plots were hatched, arrangements agreed and runs commissioned. The smugglers' pub served as a

The fifteenth-century Bell Inn, Rye's oldest pub, where smugglers stored contraband in the vaulted cellars, was linked by a tunnel to The Mermaid Inn.

meeting place, recruitment centre, secret storage facili distribution depot and valued customer.

This was nowhere more so than in the incomparable smuggli town of Rye. Riddled with linking tunnels and contraba hiding places, Rye is synonymous with Sussex smuggli Every pub was a smugglers' pub, the most famous, 1 Mermaid Inn, being frequented by the notorious Hawkhu Gang. The Mermaid was linked by a tunnel to the fifteen century Bell Inn, Rye's oldest pub, where contraband w stored in vaulted cellars with records indicating at least t raids by officials to reclaim booty.

This guide will lead you to a significant number of auther Smugglers' pubs distributed throughout East Sussex. Th wonderful old buildings with their low-beamed ceilings, fl stone floors, inglenook fireplaces and secret hiding pla give a genuine sense of the desperate days of free traders. 1 events actually occurring during the smuggling heyc provide stories every bit as wild as any to be imagined.

Alfriston
Ye Old Smugglers Inne

Waterloo Square, Alfriston BN26 5UE

Tel: 01323 870241

www.smugglersalfriston.co.uk

Stanton Collins, head of the Alfriston Gang of smugglers, lived at The Market Cross Inn, now renamed Ye Olde Smugglers Inne.

About 7 miles west of Eastbourne, Alfriston lies at the head of a valley where the Downs open out on either side to the meandering course of the Cuckmere River. This beautiful village with its 'olde worlde' charm is a magnet for visitors. With the Cuckmere flowing alongside and the coast only a mile or two beyond at the river's mouth, Alfriston was ideally placed for hiding contraband ready for transporting and distribution inland. Prior to transportation contraband was stored in extensive cellars at May's Farm.

By the late 1700s smuggling was rife and the local participants ruthless. Preventive Men patrolling the Seven Sisters cliffs marked their path with lumps of chalk, visible at night. These

Comfortable country chairs arranged round the wood burning stove in the huge inglenook stand on the ancient brick floor of the original 'Smugglers' Bar'.

Below: This unique building, with its 21 rooms, 48 doors, six staircases, various hiding places and hidden exits became the ideal headquarters for local free traders.

were easily removed causing an unsuspecting patrolman to tumble over
the edge. There are stories that on
occasion they may have been pushed.
This is the explanation given for the
death of Excise Man Thomas Fletcher
who fell to his death in 1750 and lies
buried in one of the two raised tombs
just east of Friston church.

During the Napoleonic Wars when
there was real fear of invasion by the
French, a large number of troops were billeted in the area.
This increase in population provided a number of legitimate
opportunities for making a good living. Pubs and inns prospered as did brewers, maltsters, coopers, glovers, harness
makers, shoemakers, tanners and peruke (wig) makers. The
bubble burst with Wellington's decisive victory at Waterloo
in 1815 when the population turned once again to smuggling.

Sussex ales and cider are dispensed by enthusiastic, friendly staff, knowledgeable about the inn's smuggling legacy.

The George Inn was then the pub of choice for the free trading
fraternity until landlord Richard Adams eventually lost his
licence for running a disorderly house. The foundations of

The tranquil walled garden is a perfect venue for a lazy lunch.

this splendid flint stone and half-timbered building, first licensed in 1397, date from 1250, and a network of smugglers' tunnels leads from its cellars to adjoining buildings.

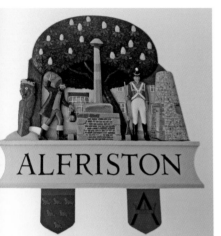

ALFRISTON

The Alfriston sign depicts a smuggler and a soldier. During the Napoleonic Wars when there was real fear of invasion by the French, a large number of troops were billeted in the area.

In 1822 Stanton Collins arrived at Alfriston to work in his father's beer house and butchers' shop near the market cross. At the time twenty-three-year-old Bob Hall was running a smuggling business from The George Inn, where a present day guest suite is named after him. The oldest part of the inn, featuring an impressive inglenook fireplace with huge copper hood, has oak floors and Sussex hop bines decorating the walls.

When The George became a respectable coaching inn, the Alfriston Gang moved their headquarters to the Cross Stone Beerhouse, later called The Market Cross Inn, now renamed Ye Olde Smugglers Inne. This unique building, with its 21 rooms, 48 doors, six staircases, various hiding places and hidden exits, became the ideal headquarters for illicit business to be run without fear of discovery.

The front bar with its old red-brick floor, heavy black beams and large inglenook is the original part of the pub. Collins lived above this room and positioned mirrors in a shaft beside the chimney to observe who was entering the bar. His accommodation provided a series of hiding places and an escape route through the loft to adjoining buildings.

Stanton Collins became leader of the banditti who included, among others, Samuel Thorncraft, Lewis Aucock, John Adams and bricklayer Richard Wilson. For years they defied the law and although many outrages were attributed to them, they plied their trade with so much cunning, corruption and connivance of the local population no real evidence was ever brought against them.

The gang broke up in 1831 when Collins was caught stealing barley from a nearby farm at Litlington. During the Winter Assizes at Lewes he was sentenced to seven years transportation. Returning to England after completing his term he was employed as a manservant to the Rector of Herstmonceux, and later promoted to footman. Bob Hall, last surviving member of the gang, died in Eastbourne Workhouse in 1895 aged ninety.

With lots of enticing nooks and crannies Ye Olde Smugglers Inne oozes character. Arranged round the wood-burning stove in the huge inglenook, comfortable country chairs stand on the ancient brick floor in the original 'Smugglers' Bar'. Since free trading days the building has been extended creating a series of small irregular rooms at various levels leading through to a conservatory, large sun trap patio and tranquil walled garden.

With the Cuckmere River flowing alongside the village, Alfriston was ideally placed for bringing contraband ashore to be hidden away prior to transportation inland.

Bull's Head

Boreham Street, Near Herstmonceux BN27 4SG

Tel: 01323 831981

www.bullsheadborehamstreet.co.uk

The seventeenth-century Bull's Head inn fronting the A271 Hailsham Road at Boreham Street began life as a farmhouse where the farmer's wife brewed beer for the farm workers. Over time it developed into an inn and the prominent bow-windowed extensions to the front and side were added as a lookout for approaching stage coaches.

Land reclamation since smuggling days means the pub now stands 4 miles inland having lost the sea views described by John Byng in the summer of 1788.

Local landowner, Edward Jeremiah Curteis (1762-1835), inherited the inn when he succeeded to his father's estates in 1806. Edward became MP for Sussex and moved to the elegant family mansion at Windmill Hill, a mile

For centuries the historic Bull's Head inn has offered a welcome to travellers.

west of Boreham Street. He experienced mounting concern over increasing smuggling caused by punitive taxation. Speaking in the House of Commons he won a reputation as a dogged defender of the agricultural interest. Realising poverty drove agricultural workers into smuggling he expressed his humanitarian concern at the forceful methods employed by the Preventive forces and requested details of the number of casualties injured in affrays with Navy Blockade Men, arguing that a reduction in customs duties would give '*an effectual check to smuggling*'.

This was the first Public House purchased by Harvey & Son (Lewes) Ltd

John Byng (1743-1813), was a countryman at heart but his tedious job as a civil servant forced him to live most of the year in London. During winter he studied old maps and travel journals planning summer excursions recorded in *Rides Around Britain*.

It is tempting to wander through the linked rooms pondering on its history.

His journal accounts are often scathing about available lodgings and food. A good experience, like the one he recorded in 1788 at The Bull's Head is rare:

'I turn'd left, as directed and soon coming into the Lewes road, walk'd my horse quietly to Boreham [Street]: here was a most tempting public house, and it was now the right hour of appetite; so I ordered the cold beef to be laid forth in a clean bow-windowed room and then I awaited at a place of wide view for my companion, who in half an hour came not; so I galloped forward, and soon heard of him on the road before me, which he had enter'd by a distant round about path.'

'When overtaken I stated to him the comforts of my past inn, and so strongly that he return'd and did not think the mile of return ill taken, when it brought to him such a neat quarter and to such nice cold beef. Our stay here was long and comfortable, all neatness within, all beauty without; our bow-window'd room commanding a fine expanse of country and the woods of Ashburnham and, to the right, views of the sea....'

The bow-windowed room where John Byng much enjoyed dining over two-hundred years ago.

During his travels Byng sometimes encountered smugglers at work. A couple of years earlier during a tour of Kent he stayed at The Anchor alehouse in Aylesford with its *'most miserable stabling'* and *'bad mutton chops'*. He declared that: *'No dinner could be worse than ours, nor could a stupider innkeeper be found! Our landlord was a surly ignorant brute'*. Byng continued, however, with a very interesting observation on the quality of horses smugglers could afford:

'We saw, whilst at dinner, a gang of well-mounted smugglers pass by. How often I wish'd to be able to purchase a horse from their excellent stables'.

Ashley, happily presenting the pub's beer range, which in addition to Harvey's Best and two seasonal Harvey's ales includes Bull's Head Bitter, specially brewed for the pub.

The road the Bull's Head faced became a notorious highway and a report of an assault by smugglers on the lame, half-blind turnpike gatekeeper and his wife appeared in the *Sussex Herald* in September 1791. A couple of hundred yards west of the pub is the former Smugglers' Wheel restaurant which has

Garden seating and a large car park now occupy a rear area previously stables and paddocks.

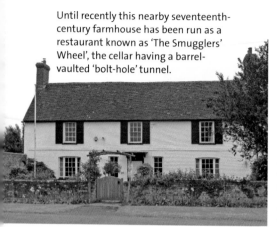

Until recently this nearby seventeenth-century farmhouse has been run as a restaurant known as 'The Smugglers' Wheel', the cellar having a barrel-vaulted 'bolt-hole' tunnel.

an internal crank wheel by the fireplace located at the head of a shaft leading down to the cellars. Tunnels leading from the cellars were known to be used by smugglers.

This comfortable old country inn with its mix of well-worn tables and chairs standing on ancient wooden floors has thankfully escaped the attention of designers, and been allowed to grow old gracefully inviting one to wander through the linked rooms while pondering on its history. There are two cellars, one accessed directly through a trap door in the bar.

Harvey's beer range includes the specially brewed Bull's Head Bitter. This gem of a genuine pub boasts a menu to please everyone. Burgers, pies, steaks and a range of seafood dishes cooked with herbs and vegetables from the pub's own garden are all included.

Boreham Street, free of traffic, as the smugglers would have known it.

Burwash Weald
The Wheel Inn
Heathfield Road, Burwash Weald TN19 7LA

Tel: 01435 882299

www.thewheelburwashweald.co.uk

Dating from around 1760, the single storey building on the right is the former stables where contraband was stored.

Burwash Weald is a village with an identity crisis, made up of two overlapping hamlets. Approaching from Heathfield you enter Burwash Common but from Burwash it is sign-posted Burwash Weald. The area was originally called Burwash 'Wheel' after its first pub *The Catherine Wheel* named after St Catherine who was martyred on a spiked breaking wheel.

In September 1788, Revenue Officer Pudsey seized 15 casks of foreign spirits and deposited them in The Wheel Inn's stables. When free traders attempted to retake the contraband Pudsey shot one in the arm before gaining assistance from a Peace Officer and securing his seizure.

The large open-plan bar featuring a massive inglenook is the hub of this handsome village pub.

This fracas was just one of a number that occurred hereabouts as the pub continued to be frequented by smugglers and other criminals. It is reported that around 1834 people as far away as Portsmouth spoke of The Wheel as the roughest pub ever. In 1896, aged thirty-one, Rudyard Kipling came to live in West Sussex at Rottingdean. This move followed an eventful early life in India, schooling in England and four years in America with his wife Caroline. The couple stayed first at North End House with Edward Burne-Jones, Kipling's uncle by marriage and later moved to The Elms across the green.

By this time Kipling had become an experienced and inquisitive journalist with an established reputation as a poet and short story writer. His deep affection for his adopted county was soon reflected in his poetry:

> *I'm just in love with all these three,*
> *The Weald and the Marsh*
> *and the Down countree.*
> *Nor I don't know which I love the most,*
> *The Weald and the Marsh or the White Chalk coast!*

In addition to Harvey's Sussex Best Bitter and Sharp's Doom Bar there is a changing guest ale on hand pump.

Leading off from the bar is a light, airy, spacious dining room where a wide selection of good value food is served seven days a week.

Fifty years earlier smuggling had flourished in and around Rottingdean with all members of society being involved or affected in some way. From older residents, with living memories of the time, Kipling absorbed stories of *'Five and twenty ponies'*, loaded with contraband trotting through the village while children were advised to turn their faces to the wall *'...while the Gentlemen go by!'* His reference to *'Brandy for the Parson, 'Baccy for the Clerk'* originated from tales about the Rev'd Thomas Hooker, vicar of Rottingdean from 1792 to 1838, who took an active part in these clandestine events.

In 1902 the Kiplings swapped the *'White chalk coast'* for *'The Weald and the Marsh'* and the tall-chimneyed, Jacobean

Rudyard Kipling painted in 1899 by Sir Philip Burne-Jones, son of the Pre-Raphaelite artist Sir Edward Burne-Jones and his wife Georgiana Macdonald.

Courtesy of the National Portrait Gallery

mansion called Bateman's, located half a mile south of Burwash village. Kipling later wrote about his impression when first looking over the house saying he felt *'her spirit – her Feng Shui – to be good. We went through every room and found no shadow of ancient regrets, stifled miseries, nor any menace though the "new" end of her was three hundred years old.'*

In 1906 Kipling completed *Puck of Pook's Hill*, his attractive collection of historical poems and stories, ostensibly for his and other children. The book shows his empathy for the place where he had chosen to settle and, with the inclusion of *A Smugglers' Song*, it demonstrates his deep understanding of the former free trading way of life throughout Sussex.

Bateman's, was home to the Kiplings until Rudyard's death in 1936. It is now cared for by the National Trust as a memorial to the author and open between April and October when it is possible to visit his study and stroll across the lawn with its view of Pook's Hill.

Bateman's (N.T.), the tall-chimneyed, Jacobean mansion, a half mile south of Burwash, was the home of Rudyard Kipling and his family from 1902 until 1936. It was here in 1910, he wrote, *A Smugglers' Song* which remains the definitive description of free trading.

From *A Smugglers' Song*

IF you wake at midnight, and hear a horse's feet,
Don't go drawing back the blind, or looking in the street,
Them that ask no questions isn't told a lie.
Watch the wall my darling while the Gentlemen go by.

Five and twenty ponies,
Trotting through the dark –
Brandy for the Parson, 'Baccy for the Clerk.
Laces for a lady; letters for a spy,
Watch the wall my darling while the Gentlemen go by.

The original building which became the first pub was built in the thirteenth century but later converted to a poorhouse. The present pub was built about 1760, around the same time the hamlet was renamed Burwash Weald.

Set in a large beer garden The Wheel Inn is light, airy and spacious inside and as far removed from its earlier derogatory description as can be imagined. The main part is the large open-plan bar featuring a massive inglenook. In addition to Harvey's Sussex Best Bitter and Sharp's Doom Bar there is a varying guest ale. Leading off from the bar is a separate dining room where a wide selection of good value food is served seven days a week. The adjoining single storey function room was formerly stables where contraband was stored.

Burwash
Rose & Crown

The Ham Lane, Burwash TN19 7ER

Tel: 01435 882600

www.theroseandcrownburwash.co.uk

Burwash is the perfect example of a peaceful picture postcard village appearing to pose for the camera, showing its most flattering aspect. Everything is as it should be; there is a sense of harmony in the way the well conserved cottages curve along the High Street. But there are clues to an earlier time when things hereabouts were not as tranquil.

The area around Burwash was central to the Wealden iron industry which used ironstone from various clay beds and was fuelled by charcoal made from trees in the heavily wooded landscape. A large proportion of the bar iron made in England in the sixteenth century, and used in most British cannon until about 1770, was produced in the Sussex Weald.

This old tile-hung local is tucked away down a lane off the high street in the heart of this lovely village.

Real ale from Harvey's of Lewes is offered by experienced French landlady Mireille Fabier, (right).
Below: There are cosy log-burning stoves in both restaurant and bar.

A serious decline in the early nineteenth century was due to competition from the North of England whose furnaces were fuelled by coke processed from coal.

When the Wealden industry began to collapse the unemployed took to smuggling and highway robbery. By the time free trading had reached its height the whole area was plagued with gangs of smugglers and criminals with the bulk of its inhabitants considered to be ignorant and lawless.

Excellent food is served in the bar and in the thirty-seater character restaurant.

A line of pollarded lime trees, signifying a safe haven for smugglers, still shades high street properties with names like Smugglers' Cottage and Revenue Cottage where access through adjoining roof spaces provided an escape route.

From an informer John Boxhall (or Boxwell), a member of the Hawkhurst Gang, we learn that 15 cwt of tea had been landed in 1740 between Hastings and Bulverhythe. The contraband was taken to a barn in Etchingham, about 2 miles west of the Rose & Crown while the smugglers refreshed themselves and retired to bed.

Thomas Carswell, Custom House Riding Officer and a party of Preventive Men discovered the tea and, supported by a

In addition to the pretty side garden there is also this covered back terrace.

number of dragoons, began to escort it back to Hastings in a waggon. Word got out to the smugglers who rallied attacking the convoy at Robertsbridge killing Carswell and seriously injuring one of the dragoons. Eight men were convicted and eventually executed for their part in the murder of Thomas Carswell.

Today St Bartholomew's church stands serene near the war memorial with bucolic views from the churchyard across the Sussex Weald. However, in the writings of Reverend John Coker Egerton, curate and rector of Burwash (1857-1888), this is shown to be an illusion. The clergyman reveals that a former Sussex parson feigned illness for a whole Sunday on suddenly hearing in the morning that smugglers, hard pressed by the Revenue, had desperately lodged a cargo of contraband among his pews. Things were no better however, in the middle of the nineteenth century. Writing in 1869, Mr

The village sign reflects the former importance of the iron industry to Burwash.

Trower recorded it had been unsafe to travel along the Heathfield turnpike between 1820 and 1840 for fear of robbery from vagrants.

The old tile-hung Rose & Crown is tucked away down a lane off the high street in the heart of this lovely village. Parts of the pub, dating from Tudor times, are endowed everywhere with historic timbers plus a glass-covered internal well just inside the entrance.

Although the pub has a large open-plan layout it feels, today, surprisingly intimate with low ceilings and two cosy log-burning stoves. Upright timbers divide the interior into separate dining areas with quirky corners. Excellent food is served in the thirty-seater restaurant under the watchful eye of Mireille Fabier, the experienced French landlady. Children and dogs are welcome inside, and outside in the pretty garden and back terrace. Real ale is from Harvey's of Lewes.

A line of pollarded lime trees signifying a safe haven for smugglers, still shades a row of high street properties with names like Smugglers' Cottage and Revenue Cottage.

Developed from three iron workers' cottages built around 1430, the Hatch has been a pub for 300 years.

Coleman's Hatch
The Hatch Inn

Kidds Hill, Colmans Hatch TN7 4EJ

Tel: 01342 822363

www.hatchinn.co.uk

Ashdown Forest was established as a royal hunting ground soon after the Norman conquest of England. By 1283 it was fenced in by a 23 mile 'Pale' – a ditch and bank with a wooden fence on top to prevent deer escaping. The pale, which enclosed 20 square miles, had 34 gates and hatches at intervals. Still remembered today in place names such as Coleman's Hatch and Chelwood Gate these entrances allowed locals access to graze livestock, collect firewood and cut heather and bracken for animal bedding. This activity established forest trails, later used by smugglers transporting contraband from the coast to eager customers in London.

The forest was the centre of a nationally important iron industry during the Roman occupation of Britain. The skill was re-established in the Tudor period when England's first charcoal-fuelled blast furnace was built in 1496 at Newbridge near Coleman's Hatch. When more efficient coke fired furnaces were established in Northern England the Sussex industry declined forcing many locals to turn to smuggling to feed their families.

Appreciative patrons can sample beers from Young's, Larkins and Harvey's.

Smugglers' Lane, north of Crowborough, was part of the inland route for London-bound contraband. In June 1743 a consignment of tea and brandy was brought ashore between Bexhill and Pevensey. James Blackman, innkeeper at the village of Hooe (see page 69) escorted armed, mounted convoys on their next stage to contraband hiding places on the Ashdown Forest.

Inside the ancient inn, low beams, candles and fireplaces create a warm and welcoming atmosphere.

At Wych Cross, the highest point on the road near Forest Row, convoys would stop and set down their burdens for a

The Hatch Inn is a comfortable, convivial place to meet for a drink or a meal.

The Ashdown Beer Festival is held here in early summer when views across the Forest from the two large beer gardens are especially fine.

welcome break. After resting undisturbed they continued along the new turnpike road through East Grinstead and Felbridge on what is now the A22 towards the capital via Godstone.

Ashdown Forest provided excellent temporary storage for goods landed elsewhere in East Sussex. There are known to have been hiding places near the lakes in Sheffield Park,

among well recognised clumps of trees and near the villages of Buxted, Fairwarp, Duddeswell and Nutley. The Hatch Inn tucked away at Coleman's Hatch certainly would have been well known and used by free traders.

In the 1780s, when smuggling was at its height in the area, Mr Walter, the local Chief Revenue Officer recruited paid spies, and together with his assistants Mr Hubbard and Mr Jenden trained a detachment of twenty dragoons to act on information received. Walter was particularly successful in capturing goods being transported for concealment in the forest. The seizures continued over a three year period and during one particular month his men captured 2½ tons of tea, although this was a mere fraction of what was getting through.

Smugglers Lane, Crowborough was a southern entry to the Forest for contraband convoys travelling up from the coast.

Free traders temporarily stashed contraband in concealed areas near forest clumps such as this one seen from 'Smugglers picnic stop' car park.

The Hatch Inn, is a picture perfect English country pub developed from three iron workers' cottages built around 1430, and has been a pub for nearly 300 years. Inside low beams, candles and fireplaces create a warm, welcoming atmosphere which draws an appreciative crowd to sample beers from Young's, Larkins and Harvey's.

Proprietor, Nicholas Drillsma and partner Sandy Barton have built an enviable reputation over twenty years in producing the highest quality, locally sourced food, complemented by an extensive wine list including ten wines served by the glass. The Ashdown Beer Festival is held here in early summer when views across the Forest from two large beer gardens are especially fine.

The Smugglers picnic stop car park at Wythiam, 3 miles west of Coleman's Hatch.

The Tiger Inn, East Dean stands at the edge of the village green where in summer life spills onto the sun-soaked terrace.

East Dean
The Tiger Inn
The Green, East Dean BN20 0BY

Tel: 01323 423209

www.beachyhead.org.uk/the-tiger-inn

East Dean, a small attractive village close to the coast at Birling Gap, lies about 5 miles west of Eastbourne in a steep valley, well hidden in the South Downs surrounded by pretty farmland. Listed as 'Esdene' in the Domesday Book, the name of this ancient settlement means 'the East Valley'.

From the cliff tops at Birling Gap access down to the former contraband landing beach is via a metal staircase. Smugglers used ropes and large wicker baskets to lower men down and haul goods up.

Down a step to the right of the bar is a cosy small room with a high-backed settle and some nice old chairs around wooden tables on carpeting.

A varying guest beer is offered alongside Harvey's Best and the truly local Long Blonde from Litlington brewery.

In 1750 Excise Man Thomas Fletcher fell to his death when patrolling the Seven Sisters cliffs. One of a number of Preventive Men who died this way, he lies buried in one of two box tombs just east of St Mary's church at Friston. Patrolling Officers habitually marked the location of their beat with lumps of chalk, visible at night. It was a simple matter to move these and lead unsuspecting patrolmen fatally to miss their footing. On occasion they may also have been pushed.

A contemporary newspaper reported it was quite common to see a dozen smuggling vessels anchored off the coast in broad daylight. At Beachy Head smugglers used portable wooden derricks to hoist cargo to the cliff tops. On one dark night a coast blockader was hurrying along the beach conscious of the incoming tide when he tripped and tumbled over a smugglers basket. Caught up in the ropes he was jerked to the top of the cliff but had the presence of mind to fire his pistol, signalling his mates. The smugglers fled leaving him with the

The old pub is as popular with drinkers as with diners and the atmosphere is always chatty and relaxed.

brandy from which he drew a handsome sum in prize money. In September 1783 gangs of 200 or 300 men arrived at Cuckmere Haven twice within a weekend and defiantly carried off their goods, despite opposition and the extremely rough sea on the first occasion.

Built in 1755 by a local businessman and churchwarden James Dipperay, a large house 'The Dipperays' lies

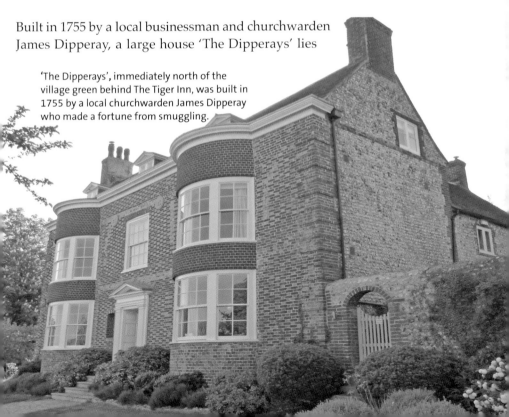

'The Dipperays', immediately north of the village green behind The Tiger Inn, was built in 1755 by a local churchwarden James Dipperay who made a fortune from smuggling.

immediately north of the village green behind The Tiger Inn. He died a rich man in 1791 having amassed his wealth from the smuggling trade through family connections with the Willard family from Crowlink, then well-known for supplying high quality duty free gin from the continent. He was also in league with his nephew who had inherited nearby Birling Manor. One story relates how James Dipperay, was once arrested but turned 'King's evidence' against his fellow smugglers thus retaining his freedom while they were transported to Australia.

When Dipperay died he left a generous bequest in his will to his gardener William Worger whose youngest son also received £1000 and 13 acres of land at Herstmonceux. Thirty years later John West and James Woolgar (possibly Worger) were Riding Officers at East Dene. So unsuccessful were they in seizing contraband an adverse report was sent to the Board of Customs. Questions remain how Woolgar, on a salary of £60 a year, shortly after was able to buy his own house and a field which still bears his name.

On one dark night a Blockade Man stumbling into a smuggler's basket on the beach was jerked to the top of the cliff together with the cache of contraband brandy.

Perfectly placed for explorers of the Sussex coast and South Downs, The Tiger Inn on the edge of a cottage-framed village

The Coast Blockade Wa-
House (far left) and w
remains of the later Coa
guard cottages at Birling G

green completes a timeless scene. Inside there is a chatty informal atmosphere, and in summer, life spills onto the terrace with visitors attracted by some of the best coastal walking in the south.

The pub is as popular with drinkers as with diners and the atmosphere is always friendly and relaxed. The focal point of the small beamed main bar is the wood-burning stove in its brick inglenook surrounded by polished horse brasses. There are, along with a few rustic benches and tables, simple wooden chairs, a window seat and a long cushioned wall bench.

Down a step to the right of the bar is a cosy small room displaying an ancient map of Eastbourne and Beachy Head. There is a high-backed settle and some nice old chairs around wooden tables on a carpeted floor. In an additional dining room to the left is a cream-coloured woodburner with traditional furniture and rugs on a wooden floor.

Excellent simple food on offer includes Beachy Head beer-battered catch of the day, the famous Tiger burger, sausage and mash with a sweet onion gravy, treacle tart with vanilla ice-cream.

Excise Man Thomas Fletcher fell to his death at Birling Gap as a result of smugglers' intervention and lies buried in the farthest of two box tombs beside Friston church. The wooden cross in the foreground, inscribed 'washed ashore', marks the communal grave of unknown persons claimed by the sea.

Groombridge
The Crown Inn

The Green, Groombridge, Kent TN3 9QH

Tel: 01892 864742

www.thecrowngroombridge.com

The pub and row of former smugglers' cottages are shaded by pollarded lime trees and overlook the steep village green just a few yards from the Kent/Sussex border.

The pretty village of Groombridge with its row of tile-hung rusty coloured cottages overlooking the steeply sloping village green lies half way between Crowborough and Tunbridge Wells. Before eventually joining the River Medway,

the little River Grom flows through the village and adjoining park, defining the boundary between Kent and Sussex.

The Groombridge Gang of smugglers was also known as 'Moreton's People'. They usually landed contraband between Hastings and Pevensey, also operating in the Romney Marsh area, both around 25 miles south of Groombridge. Goods were then moved inland to be secreted in the Ashdown Forest before being transported onward towards London around 40 miles north.

The gang rose to prominence in the 1730s led by Robert Moreton and John Bowra and there is an official record of their activities in 1733 when 30 of them were involved with moving tea inland from the marsh via Iden in a convoy of 50 horses.

By 1737 the gang was said to be terrorizing the area, and the military were sent to Groombridge to restore order. In the

The classic bar boasts an inglenook and red brick floor worn uneven over centuries.

Beers from Kent
and Sussex are on
hand pump.

same year an informer signing himself simply 'Goring'
provided a detailed insight into the gang's activities, referring
directly to an armed clash at Bulverhythe west of Hastings:

> 'This is the seventh time Morton's people have worked this
> winter, and have not lost anything but one half-hundred
> [weight] of tea they gave to a Dragoon and one officer they
> met with the first [run] of this winter.'
>
> '...When once the Smugglers are drove from home they will
> soon all be taken. Note, that some say it was [Thomas] Gurr
> that fired first. You must well secure Cat or else your
> Honours will lose the man; the best way will be to send for
> him up to London [for trial] for he knows the whole
> Company, and hath been Moreton's servant two years. There
> were several young Chaps with the smugglers who, when
> taken, will soon discover [identify] the whole Company. The
> number was twenty-six men. Mack's horses, Moreton's and
> Hoak's were killed, and they lost not half their goods. They
> have sent for more goods, and twenty-nine horses set out
> from Groombridge this day...all the men well-armed with
> long guns.'

'...I will send your Honours the Places where [you] will intercept the Smugglers as they go to Market with their goods, but it must be done by soldiers, for they go stronger now than ever.'

'...The first [run] of this winter, the Groombridge Smugglers were forced to carry their goods allmost all up to Rushmore Hill and Cester [Keston] Mark...but tea sells quick in London now, and Chaps from London come down to Groombridge almost everyday, as they used to last Winter. When once [the smugglers] come to be drove from home, they will be put to great inconveniences, when they are from their friends and will lose more Goods than they do now... Do but take up some of the servants, and they will rout the masters, for the servants are all poor.'

'Young [John] Bowra's house cost £500 building, and he will pay for looking up. Moreton and Bowra sold, last winter, some-ways, about 3,000 lb weight a week.'

The comfortable dining room is essentially welcoming.

At least eight of these men were from Groombridge itself including Moreton's servant Cat, Thomas Gurr (nicknamed Stick in the Mud), Collison, Pizon, Isaac Pope (Towser), John Kitchen (Flushing Jack), Thomas Ward (Bulverhythe Tom) and William Weston. James Blackman, landlord of The Red Lion at Hooe, was also an associate of smugglers from the villages of Rotherfield, Hartfield, Penshurst and Westerham along the route.

The lucky little girl is being treated to a birthday lunch before a visit to the children's Enchanted Forest across the road at Groombridge Place.

In 1740 the gang was implicated in the attack at Robertsbridge on Customs Men carrying seized tea to Hastings, and they continued to operate until the end of the decade, when another informer provided information leading to the round up and subsequent trial of the majority of the influential members. John Bowra was apprehended and tried but acquitted. Robert Moreton continued to lead the gang including John Barbar, Thomas Nokes, Isaac Pope and William Weston until 1749 when they were betrayed by Jerome Knapp and held at Rochester until their trial.

Little is known about the shadowy men who financed smuggling, but one wonders about William Camfield a former bricklayer from Speldhurst who turned property developer during the Tunbridge Wells building boom. By 1754 he had amassed enough money to buy the Groombridge Estate which included the whole village.

The Crown Inn stands immediately north of the border overlooking the old-cottage lined, steeply-sloping village green and is therefore technically just inside Kent. This was not an issue for smugglers of either county who happily collaborated in their nefarious work

A row of pollarded lime trees, traditionally signalling a smugglers' safe house, lines the top edge of the old village green. Completing the row of smugglers' cottages is the charming tile-hung Crown Inn, circa 1585.

This classic Wealden inn boasts old tables and a worn red-brick floor in the snug low-beamed bar with its genuine, relaxed atmosphere and adjoining small cosy rooms set up for dining. A set menu and daily specials board aim to cater for all tastes. Real ales from Sussex and Kent and Sunday roasts are specialities.

The neighbouring moated manor house of Groom-bridge Place, purchased from Chancery in 1754 by former Speld-hurst bricklayer William Camfield.

Hastings
Hastings Arms

2 George Street, Hastings TN34 3EG

Tel: 01424 722208

www.hastingsarms.co.uk

Dating from at least 1794, this atmospheric smugglers' haunt is tucked away in the Old Town back streets.

Hastings developed as a fishing port in the tenth century or earlier. Its first documented reference in 928 shows it already to be important locally, and was soon leader of the Cinque Ports – the unique association of maritime towns and villages in Kent and East Sussex, dating back a thousand years.

The town lacks a harbour and in earlier times the shingle beach had to be smoothed out manually after storms before boats could be launched by hand. Today, both tasks are performed by tractors. The history of the Hastings fishing fleet and industry is well described in the excellent free Hastings Fishing Museum on the beach.

In the mid eighteenth century the port of Hastings was more directly involved with sea than land smuggling with locals engaged in building and crewing ships which brought in the supplies. However two overland gangs did emerge, members of which undoubtedly would have convened in the Hastings Arms.

Known as 'The Hastings Outlaws' or 'The Transporters', the first gang was led by John Grayling and Jeremiah Curtis. Curtis was indicted at Lewes in 1737 before moving on to become a leading member of the Hawkhurst Gang. Grayling was sentenced to transportation but later reappeared in Sussex.

Another member of *The Hastings Outlaws*, Thomas Holman, was related to John Collier, then head of the Preventive Services (see page 64).

Hazel Sturmer and twin sister Sue run the Hastings Arms.

Collier found himself in the unenviable position of trying to protect Holman from the consequences of his involvement in a whole series of criminal activities. Following Collier's special pleading, Holman's death sentence was commuted to transportation and in fact he went abroad to live in France.

The era of the privateer, thirty years later, saw the emergence of a murderous Hastings gang known as '*Ruxley's Crew*' who earned the nickname '*Chop-backs*' after one of them split the

This quirky, unpretentious pub welcomes visitors and enjoys a great local following.

The barrel-vaulted dining room is full of interest.

spine of a Dutch sea captain. Led by the eponymous Ruxley (Stephen Bourner) they regularly boarded ships in the channel under the pretence of legitimate business. Once on board they would lock up the crew, kill any who resisted, remove the cargo and scupper the boat with all hands.

However, the gang was overpowered and beaten off whilst attacking a Dutch ship. In their haste to escape, gang member Stephen Taught was left behind. The Dutch captain decided on summary justice, and prepared to hang Taught from the yardarm. This so enraged his comrades they attacked again with renewed fervour. This time they prevailed, cut down Taught and took their revenge on the captain by slicing him down the spine.

Drunken bragging was their subsequent downfall when they boasted 'How the Dutchman wriggled when they cut him down the backbone'. An enraged Hastings population demanded to know what was to be done, and when the mayor could not offer a satisfactory reply, he was violently attacked. In response the government stationed a man-of-war offshore and assigned two hundred dragoons to the town. The gang was arrested and transferred to London for trial, since the authorities feared a local jury would be too intimidated to convict.

Mr Hodgson, landlord of the Hastings Arms in 1961, with one of the spirit containers found concealed beneath a bedroom window.

In 1961 Mr Hodgson, landlord of the Hastings Arms, discovered two old contraband hiding places. Secret cavities were revealed underneath a windowsill in a first floor bedroom and another on the landing. Inside were 3' high bespoke wooden containers linked by pipes to a tap in the bar below facilitating illegally imported spirits to be dispensed without attracting suspicion.

A prominent feature of Hasting's Fishermen's Museum, the lugger *Enterprise*, although built in 1909, is essentially similar to vessels used by old time smugglers.
Below: Vessels caught in an act of smuggling were often confiscated and sawn in half. Nets for the Hastings fishing fleet were dried and stored in the tall 'Net Shops' seen in the background.

Hastings has supported a fishing fleet for centuries but lack of a natural harbour means boats must be hauled up the shingle to the landing place at the back of the beach known as 'The Stade'.

The Hastings Arms dates from at least 1794, when it was described as *'a commercial inn of good reputation'*, serving the military personnel billeted in the town during the expected invasion by Napoleon's army.

Today this eighteenth-century smuggling haunt, tucked away in the back streets, is a warm and welcoming retreat, with scrubbed pine tables and wooden floors and walls festooned with grand mirrors and fishing nets, making it a characterful place to while away an hour or two enjoying superb Kentish ales and home cooked classics.

The fascinating history of the Hastings fishing fleet and industry is well described in the excellent free Hastings Fishing Museum on the beach.

The original timber framing of The Stag is now hidden from view behind the present neo-Georgian façade. The bar was originally on ground level and the outside steps are hardly more than a hundred years old.

Hastings
The Stag Inn

14 All Saints Street, Hastings TN34 3BJ

Tel: 01424 438791

www.staghastings.co.uk

In the ancient port of Hastings two streams flowed into the English Channel between the steep promontories of East and West Hills, causing the town to develop inwards along the valley floor.

Above the Old Town two narrow streets flank the Old London Road; the High Street and All Saints Street with The Stag Inn and ancient parish church. Burial records mention William Cruttenden and William Nash who were fatally shot on 10 Jan 1831 whilst engaged in smuggling. A landscape painted in 1811 shows just a couple of cottages north of All Saints church set in open countryside.

On the far side of The Old High Street, facing All Saints, is Old Hastings House built in 1700. This elegant Georgian town house became the home of prolific correspondent, John Collier, Surveyor General of the Customs Riding Officers for fifteen years from 1735, when he sent out more than two thousand letters that form the most important surviving account of eighteenth-century smuggling and its prevention. It was here he coordinated opposition to the violent gangs of the 1730s and 1740s.

One of these communications prompted the response, from the London Custom House on 22 Dec 1738, now on display in the bar of The Stag Inn. It relates to six Hastings smugglers: John Grayling, John Taught, John Bird, Thomas Holman, William and Nathanial Harman and contains an offer from the Commissioners of a £50 reward each for their apprehension.

Shepherd Neame ales are served with a winning smile by the landlord and his excellent team in this most friendly of pubs.

of the front bar with oden floors, black ms and ancient fire-e all contributing to nse of living history.

Found in a chimney on the first floor during the 1940s, these smoke-blackened cats may have belonged once to a witch called Hannah Clarke.

Seven years earlier the men had been sentenced to transportation for assaulting the crew of the Revenue vessel based at Rye commanded by Captain Nathaniel Pigram. The letter states the Commissioners had received information that the men:

> *'did return to England, and lurked in or near the Town of Hastings'*

and were likewise informed:

It is easy to imagine smugglers' conferences taking place in this snug back parlour.

'that on Sunday night the tenth of this Instant December, they all went on board a vessel belonging to William Gurr, of Hastings (the same in which they committed the offence for which they were Transported) to go to France for goods, in order to run them on the Coasts of Kent and Sussex.'

The Stag Inn is an Elizabethan timber-framed building with a façade altered in the mid eighteenth century. It has functioned as an inn for centuries and is thought to date from 1547 but was officially fully licensed only in 1838. Certainly it would have been frequented by free traders throughout the smuggling era.

In 1906 a hoard of George III Spade Guineas like these with a quantity of Spanish doubloons were found during repairs to the bar ceiling.

The upper storey was originally 'jettyed' projecting outward over the street, the lower storey being extended outward to bring it in line. New gables and a parapet were added to the roof, and the front elevation was plastered. The present neo-Georgian frontage consequently now hides the old timber framing.

Inside are two rooms with oak beams formed from trees already mature when Henry VIII was born. There is a front L shaped bar/dining room with another rear bar also used as a function room. Both have Tudor arched fireplaces with 1930s' brick and tile infill.

Outside is a rear patio area and a further two tiers of steeply-inclined garden.

Old Hastings House at 132 High Street built in 1700 became home for John Collier, Mayor of Hastings and diligent Surveyor General of the Customs Riding Officers.

Preserved in a glass case in the front bar are the grisly remains of two smoke-blackened cats found in a chimney on the first floor during the 1940s. It has been suggested they once belonged to Hannah Clarke, a witch said to have occupied The Stag in its early days. In 1906 when builder William McConnell was removing a front bar ceiling lining a hoard of George III Spade Guineas and Spanish doubloons tumbled out. They were covered in dust and probably secreted under an upstairs floor board sometime during the smuggling era.

Outside is a rear patio area and a further two tiers of steeply inclining garden with picnic tables below and a newly planted orchard above with a bower and a large wicker man. Like many buildings of this antiquity The Stag has an underground vault with evidence of tunnel entrances.

John Collier's Custom House is now a seafront restaurant.

Hooe
The Lamb Inn
Pevensey Marsh, Hooe Common TN33 9HH

Tel: 01424 848649

www.vintageinn.co.uk/restaurants/south-east/thelambinnpevenseymarsh

Today brick buttresses support the oldest part of The Lamb whilst acres of sheep pastures stretch away in the distance.

The Lamb Inn is located at the centre of the Pevensey Marsh, just off the B2095 about halfway between Ninfield and Pevensey. This ancient landscape is maintained by grazing livestock, mostly sheep from three local farms. 132 hectares of the marsh are owned and managed by the Sussex Wildlife Trust, as a National Nature Reserve where access is by permit only, although the Trust organises guided walks in the summer.

One of the most striking features of The Lamb is an internal contraband storage pit of the type seen in many properties in the area during the eighteenth century. Followers of the Cornish drama *Poldark* will have seen the hero excavating

Inclusion of exposed brick and timber in the recent consider-able extensions helps promote the feeling of an old country pub.

Below left: This safety cage in the oldest part of the pub highlights an intriguing secret.
Below right: One of the most striking features about The Lamb is an internal contraband storage pit of the type included in many properties in the area during the eighteenth century.

such a pit in his own house. Today, for safety reasons, a surrounding cage now replaces the original trap door.

The Lamb offers an impressive selection of real ales from Sussex and beyond.

Numerous locations close to Hooe are also known to have been used for concealing contraband. In former days when old wives' tales were believed as fact and superstition was rife, smugglers were known to spread tales of supernatural happenings to discourage locals from taking too close an interest in their activities and hiding places. Obviously this was most effective in graveyards and at Herstmonceux, 3 miles west of Hooe, goods were stored in table tombs adjacent to All Saints church.

Other hiding places were exploited among the ruins of moated Herstmonceux Castle. Here it was said a 9' tall phantom from Agincourt walked the battlements beating a drum. It would have been easy enough to reproduce the sound and perhaps even an occasional sighting, with the help of a little phosphorous!

A framed notice in the bar of The Lamb states the building is mentioned in the Domesday Book in 1084 when it was more likely a shepherd's shelter set among the traditional sheep grazing pastures. Not until 1520 did it become an inn, gaining

Outside a large brick and timber patio leads on further to a garden laid to lawn.

Contraband was stored in Herstmonceux Castle ruins 3 miles to the northwest.

a charter from the Abbot of Battle on condition that during the lambing season shepherds were allowed to warm any sickly lambs in front of the fire. This tradition continued for the next four hundred years, and even now the pub has a twentyfour-hour licence in lambing season.

Today brick buttresses support the oldest part of The Lamb whilst acres of sheep pastures stretch away in the distance. The pub was extended in the 1970s resulting in several separate spacious areas for drinking and dining. A recent stylish refurbishment of the interior, using old bricks and timbers, has very effectively reproduced the feel of a comfortable country pub.

Contraband also was said to have been secreted in the table tombs beside Herstmonceux church.

The Lamb is now a part of the Vintage Inn chain and hearty Sunday roasts and trusty British dishes head the menu, with a range just for kids offering mini versions of pub favourites. Signature Vintage pies offer fillings such as beef and merlot with buttered peas, while the 'Vintage classics' menu includes lemon and garlic-roasted chicken with seasoned chips. In the bar Sussex cask-conditioned ales are offered alongside excellent beers from further afield. Rich coffee is brewed freshly throughout the day. Outside a large brick and timber patio leads on further to a garden laid to lawn.

Hooe
The Red Lion

Denbigh Road, Hooe TN33 9EW

Tel: 01424 892371

www.redlionhooe.co.uk

The Red Lion, most authentic of Sussex Smugglers' Pubs.

Hooe village lies 3 miles due north of the contraband landing beach at Norman's Bay. Hooe's nearness to the sea, and its remoteness made the area perfect for smuggling. For generations of residents legitimate income from farming and the salt works on Pevensey Levels was substantially subsidised by free trading.

For two hundred years from the seventeenth century the nearby River Ashbourne was a major route for exporting cannons from the foundry 4 miles upstream at Ashburnham.

Some sources mistakenly claim James Blackman was the landlord of The Red Lion during the period 1733 to 1749. Born

The row of
pollarded lime
trees screening
the pub was a
'safe house' signal
to smugglers.

In this room on 10 April 1751 Riding Officer William Holland and his party failed to arrest two
smugglers and meeting with determined resistance and intimidation they were forced to withdraw for fear of their lives.

into a prominent local farming family Blackman became a successful smuggler financing and organising the local gang known as the 'The Hooe Company' who used the Red Lion as their headquarters. The landlord from 1728 was Robert Henbrey, succeeded in 1741 by his wife Martha who ran the pub for the following twelve years.

Blackman's family home was Grove House in Kiln Lane. Greatly extended today it stands behind the isolated St Oswald's church where ancestral graves can still be seen. This career criminal was also associated with both the Hawkhurst and Groombridge Gangs for whom he supervised armed convoys transporting contraband from the Sussex coast to depots in Ashdown Forest.

Landlord Leigh Harding, his wife Natalie, together with their daughter Olivia (pictured here), make the perfect pub partnership.

Fine old local photographs are on display in the back bar dining room.

Groups of rough, rude men gathered round this old fire on wet and windy nights puffing on clay pipes and discussing the next smuggling run.

Sir Cecil Bishopp of Parham House, Pulborough found himself with a problem when his daughter married Thomas Lillywhite of Storrington. Thomas was among the party of smugglers when the Hawkhurst Gang made their infamous raid on the Poole Custom House. Sir Cecil wrote pleading letters to the Duke of Richmond in his capacity as Lord Justice begging clemency for his son-in-law. Although Thomas (nicknamed Slotch in the gang) was only seventeen at the time and

A removable panel inside a bedroom cupboard reveals a hidden shaft providing access to the loft.

believed only to have been in charge of the pack horses, the aftermath of the raid was so shockingly brutal and murderous it outraged the whole country and the Duke remained unmoved.

Of the forty-odd individuals involved in the raid,

only Thomas Lillywhite was acquitted and except for one the remainder were executed or killed before the trial could take place. One smuggler was beaten to death by his accomplices 12 miles from Parham House, although his body was found dumped in the pond on Sir Cecil's estate.

Smuggling became associated with Jacobitism throughout Britain, partly due to the advantage of dealing with exiled Jacobites in France. In January 1745, before the last Jacobite rebellion, Sir Cecil's younger brother James Bishopp approached Blackman knowing of his smuggling connections. He hoped to join Bonnie Prince Charlie and urged the smuggling chief to arrange passage to France for himself, his servant and his friend James Ibbotson but apparently Blackman betrayed them and they were arrested at Pevensey.

Bales of contraband tobacco were passed up through this hole into the loft space.

A quarter sessions roll of 1751 describes an affray on 10 April, when Preventive Officers entered The Red Lion to arrest two men known to be smugglers. Riding Officer William Holland records the party met with such resistance and intimidation they were forced to withdraw for fear of their lives.

The Red Lion was built in 1495 as a farmhouse forming part of a considerable estate. In 1609 it was purchased by Elias Pattenden, a hop grower and

This rustic machine in the loft was used by smugglers to shred tobacco leaves and grind them into coarse tobacco and snuff.

brewer from Battle who was granted a six day ale and cider licence and from 1635 traded under the sign of The Red Lion.

Throughout the golden age of smuggling it became the head-quarters of the Hooe Company and contraband was regularly hidden in and around the building and bales of dried and cured tobacco leaves were taken up to the roof space to be ground into coarse tobacco and snuff. A row of pollarded lime trees screening the pub indicated to smugglers this was a safe house.

By 1805, following sufficient improvements under landlord Andrew Newton, The Red Lion was declared a 'posting house'. The large first-floor bay window was installed as a lookout for coaches and a post room set up where collected mail was sorted. For most of the nineteenth century the pub could boast a fine livery service with commodious stables. Two of the longest standing landlords at this time were black-smiths Joseph Cuthbert and William Christer.

Despite changes over the years many original features remain including hop-strung beams, flagstone floors and two big inglenooks. Generous helpings of popular home-cooked food are served and well-kept Harvey's and a guest beer are on tap. In addition to the main bar and back snug there is an overflow function room and a further dining room upstairs. Children and dogs are welcome and there are seats out front and in the garden.

The Blackman family's farm-house in Kiln Lane, with the huge nineteenth-century extension.

The seventeenth-century tile-hung Bell inn is the hub of this peaceful marshland community.

Iden
The Bell
Church Lane, Iden, Rye TN31 7PU

Tel: 01797 280242

www.thebelliden.co.uk

This pretty marshland village lies 2 miles due north of Rye. Battered gargoyles on the ancient church tower look down where the sea once rolled. Smugglers around here had their own signalling system to evade Revenue Men, possibly the origin of the name 'Owlers'. They would mimic the hoot of an owl and the cry of a rabbit. You had to be a good country-man to recognise the latter.

With the introduction of the Royal Navy Coast Blockade free trading had become a far more perilous pursuit for men from poor villages like Iden, whose fathers had relied on smuggling to survive.

Details of a smuggling run gone wrong involving the landlord and customers from The Bell Inn at Iden can be found in the fascinating record of an Old Bailey trial of 17 May 1832. William Noakes of Rye was facing the death penalty on a charge of smuggling 100 gallons of spirits and carrying offensive weapons. The transcript gives a unique insight into the logistics of assembling a large body of men at the right place and time; the hazards of a clash with an armed Preventive force; the potential for misinformation among illiterate people and the central role of the village pub.

The Bell is a quintessentially friendly village local.

On 28 January 1832 fishing smack *Seven* sailed from Rye Harbour bound for Boulogne. Charles Reynolds of Rye had

The corner by the log burner is cosy, comfortable and inviting.

The separate light dining room leads off from the bar.

organised the run and his son, also named Charles, was on board the smack. In addition to Samuel Tuggs, who turned informer, other crew members were named as Spencer, Purchase, Larkins, Tickner, Daniels and Kent.

In court, Tuggs said he helped Noakes load 170 half-ankers of spirits on board the smack in the port of Boulogne then, after spending the night loitering around the French coast, the *Seven* sailed for home on the afternoon of 30 January 1832. Back at Iden the business of organising the 'Company' of fifty to a hundred landers was underway. Certain key men were each assigned to raise small groups. Thomas Hyland, who lived at Iden, deputized Thomas Bashford, a labourer from Brookland to raise a party of ten. James Piles, another labourer from Rye, known locally as Christian, was asked to raise a group of thirty and take them to Gold's-hill-bridge and thence to Smith's Farm, a little inland from the coast and wait for orders.

The *Seven* reached Dungeness around four o'clock the following afternoon when the crew transferred the contraband into the smack's rowing boat and headed for the shore, anchoring not far from Granny Low's House and waiting for dark. Charles Reynolds senior was on the shore at Camber ready to direct operations.

The contingent of men under James Piles had walked to the beach and hid in the dunes for the better part of an hour. In the heavy sea swell the boat grounded and capsized. Two Preventive Men arrived from an eastern direction and fired into the air to raise the alarm. Three more, under the command of Captain Howard Parry, appeared from the west.

The peaceful beer garden is a popular feature in summer.

The smugglers hiding in the dunes were unarmed other than their 'bats', 7-foot long staves made from hop poles and used to threaten and beat off Preventive Men. In addition a small posse of six or so 'fire-arm men' known as the 'protecting party' were equipped with muskets. Captain Parry was badly

Contraband was brought over from Boulogne in fishing smacks like this and landed at Camber.

injured in the affray, being shot five times. One smuggler attempted to hit him over the head but the gallant Captain fired his pistol driving off his assailant.

On hearing a pistol shot the landers were told to scramble across the beach and recover the goods but they found themselves in the middle of a gun battle and some, including Noakes, attempted to run away but were forced back to the beach by the batmen. George Booth, one of the batmen tried to reassure the landers saying: *'They won't hurt you, for the firing comes from our own people'*. Less afraid, the tub carriers returned to recover the cargo, much of which was now floating in the sea. The Preventive Men seized 26 tubs but the landers managed to get the rest ashore while the boat crew escaped across the fields. In the chaos of cross firing the boatman Kent was killed.

Upwards of a hundred men would hide in the dunes waiting to assist with unloading and transportation of contraband.

When the fracas ended the party of smugglers retired to The Bell Inn at Iden where each man had been promised a pint of ale and some cheese. Tuggs made his way to the pub where he testified he saw the prisoner William Noakes, taking his

dinner. Noakes said: *'He was to have his allowance, for he had gone down and got his tubs like a man'*. Tuggs revealed he had been promised his liberty if he testified and thought there could be a reward of £500.

Bashford, another of the smugglers, was wounded and captured. He, like James Piles, hoped by giving evidence he would be freed. The final witness was Iden bricklayer Thomas Farmer, who lived near the pub. He reported seeing a party of thirty or forty men going towards The Bell around four in the morning and said: *'It was too dark for me to see if they had anything; I was at The Bell again two or three evenings after this, and saw the prisoner there.'* He testified the landlord (Thomas Allen) told him: *'They kept coming for their allowance of beer and cheese, and he did not know who should have it, and who should not.'*

'Batmen' body-guards wielding staves gave protection to the landers.

Farmer described how he had seen Noakes again on 22 March: *'There was a conversation about being taken, and he said he himself had the biggest right to be afraid for he called the fire-arm men, and went down with them and brought away a pair of tubs.'* Like the others, Farmer had seen a reward poster; *'I do not know how much it is, as I cannot read – there were three rewards; one was £200, I think – one of £1000.'* It turned out that Farmer had been paid £10 to give evidence.

It was obvious testimonies had been tainted by promises of rewards and immunities. There being no direct evidence, apart from a little hearsay, Noakes had been anything other than a batman, consequently the jury found him not guilty and he escaped the gallows.

The present pub dates mainly from the seventeenth century with Victorian additions but stands on far older foundations. Carbon dating tests on one of the beams showed it to be early twelfth century. The original building began life as a shelter for masons building the church and by the year 1210 had become a hostel with monks dedicated to the order of All

Saints brewing ale here and offering accommodation to pilgrims.

Framed on a wall in the pub is the detailed history of The Bell from 1107 to the twentieth century. From this we can see in 1726 churchwarden Crocke was granted an alehouse licence. The Bell today is a quintessentially friendly village local. They are proud of their home cooked food particularly Sunday roasts. Leading off from the bar is a separate dining room, a games area and peaceful beer garden. Functioning as a free house they serve three regular ales including Harvey's Sussex Best Bitter, Sharp's Doom Bar and 'Iden Top' from Tenterden's Old Dairy Brewery.

Outwardly The Bell Inn remains largely as the smugglers would have known it.

The Eight Bells where, during the 1780s 'Jevington Jig', head of the local smuggling gang, concealed contraband in the cellar.

Jevington
The Eight Bells
Polegate BN26 5QB

Tel: 01323 484442

www.theeightbellsjevington.co.uk

Jevington lies along the minor road between Polegate and Friston, once a busy smugglers' route. Located 3½ miles inland from the Seven Sisters the parish takes in the hamlets of Filching and Wannock to the north.

In the 1780s James Petit, who was landlord of an inn at Jevington and organised local smuggling, used a variety of aliases but was generally known as 'Jevington Jig'. His gang landed contraband at nearby Birling Gap and below Crowlink, still called Smugglers' Bottom. Birling Gap has suffered from coastal erosion and the beach is now approached down a flight of stairs.

During the eighteenth century it was possible to access the beach at Crowlink Gap which became a smugglers' landing place. The track from Crowlink Gap led to Friston then across the Downs to other Wealden villages where major gangs were located.

A fault between the cliffs runs due south of The Eight Bells at a bend in the minor road leading from East Dean to Beachy Head. Landed goods were brought up the valleys to Jevington and stored in The Eight Bells' cellar and huge basement vaults in the rectory.

Although an inveterate smuggler Petit also turned to horse stealing and various other petty crimes. As a career criminal he was not particularly accomplished, spending time in jails at Battle, Horsham and East Grinstead.

Like Gabriel Tomkins of Mayfield, when compromised by Customs Officers, James Petit turned his coat at various stages in his career. By 1792 he had changed sides and was working for ten shillings a week for Mr Walter, Customs Officer at

Standing in the centre of Jevington, Thorpe Cottage (right) renamed King's Farthing, was once linked by a connecting tunnel to The Eight Bells.

Former local builder (and Jack Nicholson look-a-like) Tony White, has been running this historic pub successfully for the last six years.

The evocative rear parlour with its prominent, exquisite fireplace.
Below: A large central servery separates the main front bar/dining room from the rear.

Horsham and was contemptuously known as a 'ten shilling man'. He cooperated with the authorities in a seizure of tobacco at Newhaven and his treachery nearly cost him his life when he was chased by a mob at Lewes.

Petit probably regarded collaboration as a last resort and was certainly resourceful in avoiding this undesirable option. On one occasion when his inn was encircled by the authorities he disguised himself in women's clothing and in a display of theatrical hysterics rushed from the building. Only his heavy boots showing beneath his petticoats gave the game away. In 1799 he stole one horse too many and was once again convicted but this time transported to Botany Bay.

This bricked-up corner of the pub cellar seals the tunnel entrance that led under the road to Thorpe Cottage.

The Jevington gang left their mark on buildings in the village. The Eight Bells and the nearby King's Farthing (formerly known as Thorpe Cottage) were both built in the eighteenth century and regularly involved in the smuggling trade. There was once a tunnel linking The Eight Bells (then a private house) to Thorpe Cottage while other reports suggest it continued to the nearby church where tombs in the church-yard were reputedly used to store contraband.

Across the road from the church and a little south of The Eight Bells, Jevington Rectory's large cellars provided convenient

Jevington Rectory has huge cellars that formerly provided convenient contraband storage facilities.

Outside, is a barbeque area and large well presented garden with lovely views of the South Downs.

storage facilities where, until fairly recently, excise marks could be discerned. The beautiful Filching Manor, less than a mile north of the pub, hides a subterranean passage leading away from its cellars and a concealed drawing room cupboard.

Heavy oak beams characterise the three-hundred-year-old Eight Bells Inn lying at the heart of this small smuggling village. A large central servery with a bar/dining room dominates the front area and an evocative rear parlour features an exquisite fireplace.

Former local builder Tony White took on the pub as a retirement project six years ago and is now working harder than ever before. Four well-kept local ales and good value seasonal food are on regular offer. Outside is a barbeque area with lovely views of the South Downs, and a large well-presented garden, including a barn and sheltered terrace for dining.

Filching Manor, north of Jevington, hides a subterranean passage leading away from its cellars, and a concealed drawing room cupboard.

The Rose & Crown was headquarters of the Mayfield Smugglers' Gang in the early 1700s.

Mayfield
The Rose & Crown

Fletching Street, Mayfield TN20 6TE

Tel: 01435 872200

www.roseandcrownmayfield.co.uk

Mayfield is a large village off the A267, 9 miles south of Tunbridge Wells. Along the beautiful High Street with its raised red brick pavements a village sign shows the figure of a young woman and children in a flowery meadow, illustrating the Saxon origin of the village name, Maghefeld, or Maid's Field.

Victorian poet Coventry Patmore called Mayfield 'The sweetest village in England' and much of it today is classed as a conservation area. The High Street alone boasts forty listed buildings of special historical or architectural importance. The parish as a whole contains nearly 180 such buildings includ-

This most interesting pub occupies three former cottages.
Below: Heavy beams, bare boards and inglenooks abound in this lovely old country pub.

ing The Rose & Crown in Fletching Street which leads down from the High Street's eastern end.

A powerful smuggling company flourished here in the early eighteenth century working in league with gangs from Groombridge and Hawkhurst. These Mayfield banditti were led by Gabriel Tomkins, otherwise known as Kit Jams, Jarvis and Uncle. Other gang members included Thomas Bigg, Francis Norwood, Jacob Walters and William Wellar. They landed contraband along the length of the Sussex coastline, and into Kent with favourite haunts including Lydd, Fairlight, Hastings, Eastbourne, Seaford and Goring.

The interior throughout is clean, bright and inviting.

In 1777 Tomkins was suspected of the murder of a Riding Officer and his fellow gang members were scarcely less desperate. When two of their number were captured at Dungeness and temporarily held in the George Inn at Lydd, the Mayfield smugglers charged up the stairs firing their pistols and releasing the pair. Tomkins himself was wounded in this famous affray.

Faced with opposition on the contraband landing beaches the Mayfield Gang generally preferred to restrain adversaries, rather than beating them senseless. At one point Gabriel

There are picnic sets on the front terrace.

Tomkins' half-brother was wanted for tying up a Customs Officer on Seaford beach during a run, and on another occasion on Goring beach the whole gang tied up a Preventive Man, throwing him into a ditch for good measure.

Gang members were caught several times but narrowly evaded conviction. They frequently won the sympathy of a local magistrate, who dismissed cases, sometimes even ordering the imprisonment or flogging of the arresting officer. Behind bars the Mayfield smugglers often found ways of securing freedom through rescue attempts or by bribing gaolers.

Gabriel Tomkins himself was first brought to justice in 1721, on his capture at Nutley after a chase from Burwash. Though he bribed his gaoler and escaped he was caught again and stood trial in London. On conviction he was sentenced to transportation but turned King's Evidence, providing much useful information in return for his freedom.

At liberty for eight years he was rearrested in 1733. This time, giving evidence to a Parliamentary Enquiry into Frauds and

Now a private house, the former Carpenters Arms alehouse stands opposite Smugglers' Lane.

Abuses in the Customs Service. His testimony suggested the organisation was riddled with corruption, resulting in the dismissal of thirty officers. This created a number of important vacancies, several of which, during the following six years, were filled by Tomkins himself, although he had admitted to having smuggled 11 tons of tea and coffee in a year – a classic instance of 'Poacher turned Gamekeeper'!

However, old habits die hard, and in 1741 Tomkins slipped quietly out of his job to resume former activities on the wrong side of the law. In 1746 he robbed the Chester Mail, and the following year helped the Hawkhurst Gang in a robbery at Selborne in Hampshire. It was the mail robbery, however, that proved his undoing. Tomkins' long and chequered career ended on the gallows on 23 March 1750.

Reminders of smuggling days in Mayfield include a curious tall house part way down the left side of Fletching Street resembling a layer cake with masonry at ground level, half-timber and brick above, then clapperboard and tiles up to the roof. It was cleverly equipped with two cellars in order to fool the Excise Men and today is divided into 1 and 2 Charity Cottages but during the Mayfield Gang era it was known as 'Maynards' after the owner doctor, reputed to be a friend of the smugglers.

This smugglers' trail was a regular trade route for carrying goods inland.

A little further down the hill the former Carpenters Arms stands opposite a track known as Smugglers' Lane. This overgrown footpath, leading downhill beside a white clapperboard house, was a regular trade route for conveying contraband goods inland.

Charity Cottages 1 and 2, formerly known as Maynards were cleverly equipped with two cellars to fool the Excise Men.

When the Mayfield smugglers gathered at this pretty sixteenth-century weather boarded pub it occupied only one cottage but has since expanded into all three in the row. Two cosy front bars with low ceiling boards and bench seats built in to partly panelled walls provide much character. There is also a small dining area behind the servery and a larger traditional dining room. Stripped floor boards and an inglenook log fire immediately convey an impression of antiquity.

Traditional hospitality from this lovely old country pub includes fine freshly prepared food with locally sourced ingredients along with Harvey's Best Bitter or a guest Sussex ale and a selection of wines by the glass. There are picnic sets on the front terrace.

A pub lunch on a perfect summer's day in Mayfield – no wonder they're smiling.

The Star was formerly The Sluice House.

Norman's Bay
The Star Inn
Pevensey, East Sussex BN24 6QG

Tel: 01323 762648

www.thestarinnnormansbay.co.uk

Norman's Bay, between Bexhill and Pevensey, is surrounded by marshland where drainage of the area began soon after the Norman Conquest. One of the earliest records dated 1180 shows 'a new marsh had been created'. In 1396 the Commissioners of The Sewers of Sussex created a new 'cut' at the sea which proved to be only a temporary solution. However in 1402 the River Ashburn was successfully diverted to run out to the sea at Normans Bay.

'Wallers Haven', the artificial channel running by the Star Inn flowed through lands previously owned by Steven Waller of Hooe. Flood gates were erected and Wallers Haven Sluice was established with a 'Sluice House' to accommodate men

Flowing beside the pub the River Ashburn is known at this point as Wallers Haven.

controlling the water rushing down from Ashburnham at high tide when the sea threatened marsh defences.

The original 1402 Sluice House is The Star Inn of today and the earliest documentary evidence of its conversion to an inn is contained in a deed of 1597. When the river was diverted to the sluice it created a small port and documentary evidence shows it was well established by 1607. Maps and drawings

The forest of black roof beams gives a clue to the antiquity.

of 1700 show The Star Inn much the same as it appears today. It was known then as 'The Star of Bethlehem', almost certainly because it was frequented by shepherds.

Eight miles up-river the famous Ashburnham ironworks forged cannons for the Admiralty. Guns brought down in barges to the sluice were taken on to Hastings for shipment to the Royal Naval Dockyard at Chatham.

Illegally exported wool from thousands of sheep on the marshes was already big business for local free traders intent on avoiding excise duties. However, the smuggling of guns to Britain's traditional enemy France, and later to Holland proved more profitable. Years later cannons captured from the French and Dutch were found to have been made at Ashburnham.

By the mid eighteenth century the largest profits were derived from importing and distributing contraband shipped from France. The local gang of smugglers was organised and led

The décor and furnishings throughout are contemporary, with high-back black leather chairs arranged around modern stylish tables.

by a family from the nearby village of Little Common, now part of the urban spread of Bexhill. The marsh offered extra protection against patrolling Preventive Men lacking local knowledge for safe crossing, particularly at night.

The gang numbered about thirty resolute men but could call on ten times that number. Records show they owned two smuggling luggers, *The Long Boat* and *The Princess Charlotte*. These were large vessels with a cargo capacity for hundreds of tubs of brandy. When not at sea they were concealed close to the lonely Star Inn at a secret location near Wallers Haven known locally as 'Willow Tot'.

Normans Bay beach where tons of contraband were landed by the smugglers of Little Common.

The biggest challenge to smugglers operating from The Star Inn was Captain John Clark, Commanding H.M. Revenue Cutter *Vulture* based at Newhaven. It was a fast boat with a cannon on its bows and more than a match for a lug-sail boat weighed down with a cargo of spirits. Captain Clark knew

about eighty per cent of the contraband landed between Newhaven and Hastings, was coming ashore at Normans Bay.

On 21 October 1805, when patrolling off Beachy Head, Captain Clark noticed a large, heavily-laden lug-sail boat heading for the bay. Giving chase he successfully captured the crew and 540 casks of fine brandy worth 5/- a gallon. Just over three months later, on 6 January 1806, he captured another lugger only a mile off from The Star Inn with 500 parcels of tea on board, worth 28/- a pound in England.

The free trader's luck finally ran out on 13 February 1822 when three hundred of them, armed with cudgels and poles, gathered in front of The Star Inn. Close inshore a light flashed from *The Princess Charlotte* but before the ship made landfall, an armed party of Preventives arrived and breaking up the gathering with gunfire, shot one of the smugglers in the process.

The Star Inn much as the Little Common smugglers would have known it.

Contemporary reports in the *Sussex Advertiser* claim the Norman's Bay sluice was the very last stronghold of smuggling in the county, continuing right up until 1832. Locally it is known the gang was still operating as late as 1850.

The last recorded run began on the night of 3 January 1828, ending in one of the bloodiest fights in the history of Sussex smuggling. Two hundred smugglers landed the cargo and made off with it inland. At Sidley Green they were blockaded by forty armed Customs Men but fought their way through leaving their dead behind and taking their wounded with them on the contraband carts.

One of those killed was an old smuggler named Smithhurst who was found still clutching his wooden cudgel. At the subsequent Old Bailey trial ten men were sentenced to death but later transported. The price they paid in punishments and blood was now too great and until 1850 they concentrated on relatively small runs before giving up completely to follow respectable occupations.

A signposted footpath beside the formerly isolated inn marks the riverside track regularly used to carry contraband inland.

Although part of The Star Inn is over 500 years old the only interior signs of antiquity are the solid stone walls and forest of heavy black roof timbers. The décor and furnishings throughout are contemporary with high-back black leather chairs arranged around modern stylish tables. Best described as a family eatery, The Star offers a large selection of good value dishes. Harvey's Best and a guest ale are on tap.

Outside are extensive gardens including children's safe play areas. Despite an adjacent small development of park homes it is possible to appreciate how isolated this spot once was. A signposted footpath running beside the inn marks the riverside track regularly used to carry contraband towards the Lamb Inn and Hooe village.

Pett
Two Sawyers
Pett Road, Pett Village TN35 4HB

Tel: 01424 812255

www.twosawyers.co.uk

The small, peaceful, coastal village of Pett, between Rye and Hastings, perches on a high ridge overlooking Pett Level and lies alongside the western end of a sea defence wall from the top of which are wonderful views of the sea, beach and cliffs. Pett Level has a fragile hold on the land, with a sense of transience about its very existence, as if the sea will eventually have its way and occupy the land, continuing a process thousands of years old.

Although expanded in recent years, evidence of the ancient settlement can still be seen in a number of old village buildings including the Two Sawyers, mentioned in the Domesday

The Two Sawyers is a beautiful sixteenth-century inn with many original features, embowered with ivy and flowers during summer.

Book as being owned by a Norman Abbot after the Battle of Hastings when William the Conqueror distributed his new possessions among supporters. The relevant passage reads:

> 'the 5th abbot of Fecamp holds for the King the house called Sawyers in the Guestling Hundred.'

A lease of 1737 describes the Two Sawyers as a wayside cottage owned by Abraham Martin. It was later a butcher's shop and a forge, and by 1788 was owned by James Easton and trading as an alehouse run by Thomas Harman of Fairlight.

The bare-boards bar leads to a snug dining room beyond.

The pub's name implies the possibility of a previous timber business nearby. Various historians have referred to the surge of new construction and re-modelling of local houses during the sixteenth and seventeenth centuries' as 'The Great Rebuilding'.

An ancient form of woodland management provided charcoal for Sussex iron furnaces and oak for timber-framed buildings characteristic of the region. These businesses afforded a perfect cover for the transportation of contraband. The pub sign depicts two men 'logging'. Before the introduction of sawmills, all timber was cut by hand usually close to where it was felled. The more difficult 'planking' was undertaken in specially constructed sawpits, in which two sawyers, one in the pit (the pitman) and one above (the topman), cut the timber with two-handed saws, examples of which are displayed in the pub. Accomplished and proficient sawyers, however, were classed as unskilled workmen and forbidden entry into the guilds of carpenters, joiners and shipwrights. This was an added incentive to become involved in smuggling.

A narrow passage slopes downward to the restaurant with open fireplace and a two-handed saw displayed on the inglenook beam.

Smugglers' landing beaches stretched from Rye along Pett Level to Fairlight cliffs east of Hastings. Contemporary maps show carts could be taken down to the Fairlight Cove beach.

The friendly bar is the hub of this popular pub.

Some accounts of smuggling here distinguish between episodes at Fairlight Steps and those at Covehurst or Govers Bay which were used particularly by owlers. Later coastal erosion and large landslides have substantially altered the coastline here, making the former inaccessible and others difficult to reach on foot.

The history of smuggling in and around Pett continued through a century and a half and Toot Rock in Pett Level was a recognised meeting place for free traders. On one moonless night several smugglers drowned in the Royal Military Canal near Pett when they failed to find the recognised fording place.

In addition to the front courtyard suntrap there is an extensive back garden with shady trees and well-spaced tables.

As one meanders through low-beamed rooms in this beautiful sixteenth-century inn many original features are revealed. The bar with bare boards and stripped tables is the hub. From here a tiny snug passage slopes downward to a restaurant with an open fire and other dining areas are tucked away amongst historic rooms boasting fine oak support beams and a large collection of early saws.

Smugglers knew this building before thatch gave way to roof tiles.

Pett Level, with its fragile hold on the land, faces the continuing process of erosion thousands of years old.

This very friendly pub specialises in popular good value freshly-made food. Beers include Harvey's Best and guests like Southern Belle from Cottage Brewing Company and Fortyniner from Ringwood plus local farm cider and perry and a wide range of wines.

These former Coastguard cottages are now private homes.

Children are welcome in the restaurant and the bar is dog friendly. The large beer garden is a delight in the summer with a profusion of shady trees and well-spaced tables. Additional seating is also available in a covered decking area at the rear. A suntrap formed by a brick paved front courtyard is enclosed by a centuries old rustic brick wall resplendent with hanging baskets and hydrangeas in profusion.

Fairlight Cove was a favourite landing spot where carts could be taken down to the beach.

Pevensey
The Smugglers

High Street, Pevensey BN24 5LF

Tel: 01323 762112

www.smugglerspevensey.co.uk

A great sweep of shingle beach links Norman's Bay in the east with Pevensey Bay in the west. In Saxon times Pevensey was the largest natural harbour along the whole of the south coast but eastward drift of tides and storms from the west, gradually formed a shingle bar across the bay. Eventually this prevented inland waters of the River Ashburn reaching the harbour and the sea. Centuries of silting up resulted in Pevensey losing its port and its importance.

Originally called the New Inn, the name of the pub was changed to acknowledge its involvement with the free trade and its participants.

Today Pevensey appears almost abandoned on a spur of sand and clay, about 10 metres above sea level. In Roman times this spur was a peninsula projecting into marshes creating a tidal lagoon. A small river, Pevensey Haven, now running along the north side originally would have discharged into the lagoon which once extended inland as far north as Hailsham and eastwards to Hooe.

The pub, dating from 1527, dominates the single village street.

The floor of the bar is made from ancient elm boards and the ceiling is supported by a massive beam salvaged from a sailing ship.
Below: The comfortable restaurant is located in the oldest part of the building.

Evidence of Pevensey's former importance as a medieval commercial centre lies in the fact it had its own mint. The much restored Mint House still stands in the single village street along with The Smugglers and the Court House which also served as the village lock up. One of the last people incarcerated here was Betty Breach whose husband Billy frequently lingered too long in the New Inn. One night she went to the inn, emptied the remainder of Billy's drink over his head and smashed the glass on the floor. The magistrate who jailed her for this offence found public opinion so much against him he not only relented but released her in person because she refused to leave the lock-up until he did so.

Real ales are from Shepherd Neame's Faversham brewery.

Throughout the eighteenth and early nineteenth centuries Pevensey Bay flourished anew, being one of the easier places for landing contraband. The Mayfield and Groombridge Gangs who rose to prominence in the 1730s landed goods

In summer music events are held in the pub's spacious garden.

here. Flushing Jack, Bulverhythe Tom, Towzer, Old Joll, Toll, The Miller, Yorkshire George and Nasty Face were among those who humped kegs and bales off the beach or acted as 'batmen', the cudgel carrying bodyguards.

The last and worst battle here took place in November 1833. The landing on Pevensey shore was spotted by Coastguards, and the unloading this time was carried out under the protection of armed smugglers who maintained a constant barrage of gunfire. For two hours a running fight ensued as the Preventive Men chased the free traders for 6 or 7 miles inland. Finally, three smugglers were killed and five taken prisoner. None of the Coastguards was injured, and each was later awarded twenty pounds in prize money. The remaining smug-

COURT HOUSE MUSEUM AND GAOL
BUILT IN TUDOR TIMES AS THE TOWN HALL
UNTIL 1886

COURT ROOM, CELLS AND EXERCISE YARD.
CINQUE PORT SEAL - PEVENSEY FROM THE ROMANS TO 1945.
FASCINATING BYGONES IN THE ROBING ROOM ETC
"PACKED WITH INTEREST"
OPEN EASTER WEEKEND AND SUNDAYS FROM APRIL UNTIL MID OCTOBER
MAY TO SEPTEMBER WEDNESDAY TO SUNDAYS INCLUDING
BANK HOLIDAYS MONDAYS 11AM - 4PM

The Court House, opposite the pub, also served as the village lock up where smugglers were held awaiting trial.

glers escaped under cover of the marsh fog, leaving a trail of blood as they headed for safe houses in Wartling and Boreham Street.

Traces still remain of those desperate days in addition to contraband hiding places in the ruins of both Pevensey and Herstmonceux Castles. Evidence of specially devised hides used over long periods can still be found. At Montague, a private house in Hankham close to Pevensey Haven, there is an elaborately constructed concealed entrance to a shaft and deep underground tunnel.

Originally called the New Inn, the name of the pub was changed to The Smugglers acknowledging its involvement with the free trade and its participants. The building dating from 1527, contains a 12 by 20 foot cellar where, it is said, tunnels led off west to the church and south to the castle. The pub comprises of two very large rooms. The floor of the

A ruin well before the smuggling days, Pevensey Castle's crumbling turrets provided convenient hiding places for contraband brought ashore at Pevensey Bay.

bar is made from ancient elm boards and the ceiling is supported by a massive beam salvaged from a sailing ship. The restaurant is located in the oldest part of the building, both boasting open fires.

As well as steaks, salads and pub classics The Smugglers specialises in fish dishes such as homemade fish pie made

The beach at Pevensey Bay was one of the easier places to land contraband and the Groombridge Gang in particular made good use of it.

from salmon, cod and king prawn in a spinach & cheese sauce topped with celeriac mash and vegetables. Other favourites include pan fried sea bass fillets with chilli, ginger & spring onion on a bed of crushed potatoes and Cajun spiced tuna steak with mango salsa. Real ales are from Shepherd Neame's Faversham brewery.

This very welcoming, splendid old coaching inn stands prominently at the top of the steep High Street.

Robertsbridge
The George Inn
High Street, Robertsbridge TN32 5AW

Tel: 01580 880315

www.thegeorgerobertsbridge.co.uk

The village of Robertsbridge was a strategic coaching stop o the London Road, halfway between Hastings and Tunbridg Wells. Since the A21 bypass was opened in 1992 it no long has the previous vast volumes of traffic passing through i narrow High Street.

A Cistercian Abbey was founded here in 1176 and it is like that the town's name is a translation from the Latin 'Po Roberti', after the first bridge built across the River Rother the founding Abbot – Robert de St Martin. A market chart was granted in the thirteenth century and the fact th

Robertsbridge grew and prospered from that time is apparent in the number of extant timber-framed houses, the oldest dating from 1390.

Robertsbridge lay within the extended area controlled by the Hawkhurst Gang who organised local smuggling operations between 1735 and 1749. John Amos, a prominent gang member who rejoiced in the nickname 'Trip' lived in Roberts-bridge. One day he discovered that 15 cwt of tea, earlier seized by the Customs, was on its way back to Hastings under guard. Riding around the neighbourhood drumming up support for a rescue attempt he managed to assemble about thirty smugglers.

After fortifying themselves with a drink and an oath, the party set off to ambush the wagon on the steep incline of Silver Hill. The Customs Men had good cause to be nervous since the hill was notorious, and the town equally well-known for its smuggling inhabitants. The free traders launched their attack and in the ensuing battle a Customs Officer was shot dead and a dragoon seriously injured.

The elegant dining room is graced with smart contemporary furniture.

High stools stand conveniently at the bar counter where Harvey's Sussex Bitter, Sharpe's Doom Bar and a guest beer such as Native Ale from Whitstable Brewery are served.

Below: A handsome brick inglenook fireplace houses a log fire and chalk boards on the mantel shelf above inform patrons of local suppliers and daily specials.

We have to thank English art historian, man of letters, anti-quarian and Whig politician Horace Walpole, for confirmation that smugglers frequented The George. In a letter dated 5 August 1752 written to his friend Richard Bentley, Walpole made this wry observation:

'The roads grew bad beyond all badness, the night dark beyond all darkness, our guide frightened beyond all frightfulness. However, without being at all killed, we got up, or down – I forget which, it was so dark, – a famous precipice called Silver Hill, and about ten at night arrived at a wretched village called Rotherbridge. We had still six miles hither, but determined to stop, as it would be a pity to break our necks before we had seen all we had intended. But, alas! there was only one bed to be had: all the rest were inhabited by smugglers, whom the people of the house called mountebanks; and with one of whom the lady of the den told Mr. Chute he might lie. We did not at all take to this society, but, armed with links and lanthorns, set out again upon this impracticable journey. At two o'clock in the morning we got hither to a still worse inn, and that crammed with excise officers, one of whom had just shot a smuggler.'

The courtyard garden now occupies part of the old coaching yard.

Leather armchairs and a comfortable sofa are an invitation for a quiet pint and a chat.

Standing in a prominent position at the top of the steep High Street this splendid old coaching inn is very welcoming. Old wooden floors and a log fire in a handsome brick inglenook instantly convey a feeling of times past. A leather sofa and chairs by the fire present a tempting invitation for a quiet pint and a chat.

High stools stand conveniently at the bar counter where Harvey's Sussex Bitter, Sharpe's Doom Bar and a guest beer such as Native Ale from Whitstable Brewery are served, along with a farm cider and good wines by the glass. Leading off from the bar is a dining area with elegant high-backed chairs standing on stripped floor boards around a mix of tables, each with fresh flowers and tea-lights. A courtyard garden now occupies part of the old coaching yard.

Horace Walpole who, in a letter to a friend in 1752, complained all the beds in The George were occupied by smugglers.

Hilaire Belloc as a young man. In later life he became the fiercest champion of Sussex inns and Sussex ale.

Stuart Mepham, the chef, is proud of his kitchen's principle of using the best local produce sourced within 30 miles. Chalk boards on the mantel shelf inform patrons of local suppliers and daily specials. Enjoyable dishes celebrate the best Sussex and Kent produce available from tempura cod (landed at Rye or Hastings) with hand cut chips, slow roasted Gloucester Old Spot pork belly from Park Farm in Hawkhurst, or char-

grilled rib eye steaks. Stuart is also an expert photographer providing the photographs that appear on the pub's website, some of which he has kindly allowed me to use here.

One of the guest rooms in this civilised inn is named after the Anglo-French writer and champion of Sussex inns and Sussex ale, Hilaire Belloc, who stayed at The George in 1902. His famous philosophical pub crawl across the county is described in *The Four Men* beginning: '*as I was sitting in the George, at Robertsbridge, drinking that port of theirs and staring at the fire …*'

Dating from 1420, The Mermaid, is one of the best known inns in southeast England.

Rye
The Mermaid Inn
Mermaid Street, Rye TN31 7EY

Tel: 01797 223065

www.mermaidinn.com

One of the best preserved medieval towns in England, Rye is simply enchanting and has been a constant magnet for writers and artists. Perched on a hill and threaded with cobbled thoroughfares with names like Traders Passage, Lion Street and Mermaid Street, half-timbered houses and ancient inns press for space among specialist shops and cafés.

That Rye was a smuggling town for five and a half centuries is evidenced by a warrant issued in 1301 to search for: *'wool, hides, bales and all other merchandise and persons attempting to export money or silver.'* There in 1357 an Admiralty inquest was

The chimney breast above the giant inglenook is supported by a massive 20' long bressummer beam.

Below: A door in the corner of the Giant's Fireplace Bar accesses a secret staircase.

held before the deputy Lord Warden of the Cinque Ports to collect evidence against Simon Portier and several others for exporting uncustomed wool. Daniel Defoe reported watching owlers at work with dragoons and Riding Officers chasing them *'as if they were huntsmen beating up their game'*.

Following the seventeenth-century introduction of Custom duties on luxury goods fresh impetus was given to smuggling particularly along the Kent and Sussex coasts. Stories of smuggling and smugglers' pubs in Rye throughout the following century and a half could easily fill a volume on their own. In one month alone in 1745 nine smuggling cutters sailed from Rye for Guernsey: *'in order to take in large quantities of goods, to be run on the coast'*.

Established in the twelfth century on Mermaid Street, The Mermaid Inn is an institution being one of the best known inns in southeast England. The present building dating from 1420 incorporates cellars surviving from 1156 and sixteenth-century additions in the Tudor style.

In 1735 smuggling turncoat Gabriel Tomkins from Mayfield had risen to the office of bailiff for the Sheriff of Sussex by dint of information he had supplied to the Customs Board. Tomkins arrested Thomas Moore at

Rye for an offence against Revenue laws but bail was offered and accepted and Moore was discharged from custody.

Tomkins rather riskily remained in Rye on business, staying at The Mermaid Inn whose landlord at the time was Thomas Bean. One thing smugglers hate more than a Custom Officer is a traitor. Moore escorted five men to the inn, two of whom had given him bail. Together with the landlord they entered Tomkins' room seizing bail bonds and warrants against smugglers then forcing him downstairs, finally dragging him by the heels into the street. Tomkins was then taken aboard a boat to be transported overseas but when Captain Pigram, commander of the Rye Revenue sloop *Amelia*, was alerted to this he immediately sent his men to search all vessels in the harbour. They eventually found Tomkins in a state of: '*the utmost consternation*' and released him.

Harvey's Best Bitter is a permanent feature with a couple of alternating guest beers plus a fine selection of wines and malt whiskies.

There is a selective bar menu with more expensive and elaborate choices served in the exquisite linenfold panelled restaurant.

Style and comfort may be enjoyed in two separate lounges.

Throughout the 1730s and 1740s the notorious Hawkhurst Gang of smugglers, described as a *'nest of vermin'*, terrorised Kent and Sussex using The Mermaid Inn as one of their strongholds. The nineteenth-century historian of Rye, William Holloway, records he was: *'informed some years ago by a gentleman, who was born in Rye in the year 1740, that he remembered when the Hawkhurst Gang of smugglers were at their height of their pride and insolence, to have seen them (after having successfully run a cargo of goods on the sea shore) seated at the windows of this house [The Mermaid Inn] carousing and smoking their pipes, with their loaded pistols lying on the table before them.'*

The Coast Block-ade Watch House at Rye Harbour commanded the shoreline.

The Mermaid Inn is comfortable, friendly, and despite being furnished throughout with antiques is not at all pretentious. In the corner of the Giant's Fireplace Bar is a door accessing a secret staircase. The chimney breast above the giant inglenook is supported by a massive 20' long bressummer beam.

There is a selective bar menu with more expensive and elaborate choices served in the exquisite linenfold-panelled restaurant. Head

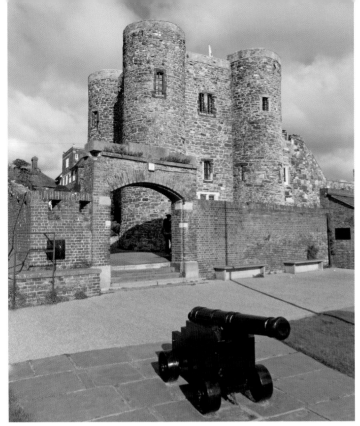

Dating from 1249 Rye Castle, also known as Ypres Tower, was built as part of the defence against the frequent raids by the French.

Part of the excellent display of smuggling history in Rye's Ypres Tower Museum.

Chef Ben Fisher is very committed to using quality, seasonal, local ingredients and cooking them to perfection. There is also the cosiness of the *Dr Syn* dining room named after Russell Thorndike's fictional smuggling parson.

Harvey's Best Bitter is a permanent feature accompanied by a couple of alternating guest beers plus a fine selection of wines and malt whiskies. Seating is available on a small outside rear terrace area.

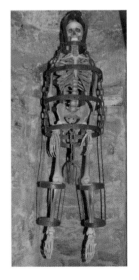

These authentic gibbet irons are on display in Ypres Tower Museum which formerly served as a prison where smugglers were frequently incarcerated. Those found guilty of murdering or injuring Preventive Officers were sentenced to death. As a fearsome warning to others, their corpses were hung in chain cages from gallows-like gibbets in prominent places on high ground or at cross roads.

The Royal Oak is a fine weather boarded building dating from 1490, a century before the Spanish Armada.

SHEPHERD NEAME

THE ROYAL OAK

Whatlington
The Royal Oak
Whatlington Road, Whatlington TN33 0NJ

Tel: 01424 870492

www.royaloakwhatlington.co.uk

In the eighteenth-century a group of Customs Officers and dragoons took refreshment here while planning to ambush a party of more than thirty smugglers.

The village of Whatlington lies divided into two parts, one in the valley on the road from Battle, where church and parish hall are separated on either side of the stream. The other is a mile or so further on the A21 where The Royal Oak pub stands at the back of the triangular village green. During the pub's early history it functioned as a coaching inn serving travellers on the Hastings to London road.

John Turner, landlord of The Royal Oak alehouse in the early 1700s was a part time member of the Hawkhurst Gang. Consignments of contraband landed at Bulverhythe were loaded onto packhorses, carried through the woods to Whatlington and secreted in 'Turner's Hole', a pit beneath the floor of a barn owned by Turner.

A report of October 1735 concerning an affray between smugglers and Revenue Men is very significant because it is claimed to be the first mention of the Hawkhurst Gang at work. It states that Thomas Pettit 'grassed' about the Hollingbourne ambush where a young man Thomas Peene was killed. Pettit claimed he heard a couple of escaping smugglers discussing their intention to hide their goods at '*Turnershole*'.

One day, in the eighteenth century a group of Customs Officers and dragoons met at the Royal Oak to plan the ambush of a local party of more than thirty smugglers. They took refreshment at the inn whilst discussing strategy but their plan ultimately was conspicuously unsuccessful because all but one of the smugglers escaped.

Kent and Sussex ales are served with a winning smile.

The Royal Oak is a fine weather-boarded building dating from 1490. The first recorded landlord was Thomas Woolett in 1509 during the reign of Henry VIII. Once part of the old stables, one room contains a medieval well 80' deep with the

Splendid open fireplaces and lots of dark beams contribute to the comfortable charm.

water level rising to 40' when full. It was uncovered by builder Roger Morgan while undertaking work for landlord Tony Cronin in 1988. This venerable building was registered as an inn in 1661 under the name of The Royal Oak, which, together with countless inns around the country, was adopted to mark the restoration of the monarchy with the return of Charles II.

Containing many dark beams the interior of this lovely old building is laid out on various levels where a splendid open fireplace exudes a comfortable charm. A spacious beer garden boasts superb views over the East Sussex countryside. Renowned for good food the traditional lunch menu includes homemade pies, ploughmans' and fish and chips with an à la carte menu using fresh, locally sourced ingredients.

The medieval well is 80' deep with the water level rising to 40' when full.

The large beer garden boasts superb views over the East Sussex countryside.